"Safety First:

How to Stay Safe During Mobs, Protests, Looters, and Flash Mobs

"Table of Contents:

Section 1: Understanding the Risks and Hazards

In today's world, unpredictable events such as mobs, protests, looters, and flash mobs are becoming more and more common. Whether you are at home, work, or out in public, you can find yourself caught up in one of these events at any time. While many of these events may start out as peaceful gatherings, they can quickly escalate into dangerous situations, posing risks to your safety and well-being.

Understanding the risks and hazards associated with these events is essential to staying safe. In this section, we will explore the common risks and hazards associated with mobs, protests, looters, and flash mobs. We will look at the causes of these events, what triggers them, and how they can escalate out of control. We will also examine the impact these events can have on individuals, businesses, and communities.

Chapter 1: Introduction to Managing Unpredictable Events

Unpredictable events can happen anywhere and at any time. They can occur due to a variety of reasons, including political, social, or economic issues. These events are not always violent, but when they do turn violent, they can be extremely dangerous. That is why it is essential to understand how to manage unpredictable events.

Managing unpredictable events involves knowing what to do when you find yourself in a potentially dangerous situation. It involves having a plan of action, knowing how to assess the situation, and taking the appropriate steps to protect yourself and others. It also involves knowing when to leave the area and how to do so safely.

In this chapter, we will explore the basics of managing unpredictable events. We will look at the different types of events that can occur, the risks associated with them, and how to assess the situation. We will also discuss how to prepare for these events, what to do when you find yourself in the midst of an event, and when it is safe to leave.

Chapter 2: Common Risks and Hazards Associated with Mobs and Protests

Mobs and protests are some of the most common types of unpredictable events that can occur. They can be triggered by a variety of reasons, including political, social, or economic issues. They can start off peacefully but can quickly escalate into violence, causing harm to individuals, businesses, and communities.

Understanding the common risks and hazards associated with mobs and protests is crucial to staying safe. In this chapter, we will explore the risks associated with these events. We will look at how they can escalate, the potential harm they can cause, and how to assess the situation. We will also discuss how to stay safe when participating in a protest or demonstration.

Chapter 3: Understanding the Risks and Hazards Associated with Looting

Looting is a form of theft that occurs during unpredictable events such as riots, natural disasters, or civil unrest. It involves breaking into buildings and stealing goods or property. Looting can be extremely dangerous as it often involves violent behavior and puts both looters and innocent bystanders at risk.

Understanding the risks and hazards associated with looting is essential to staying safe. In this chapter, we will explore the common risks and hazards associated with looting. We will look at how looting occurs, what triggers it, and how it can escalate. We will also discuss how to protect yourself and your property during a looting event.

Chapter 4: Flash Mobs: Understanding the Dangers and Risks

Flash mobs are a form of social media-driven gathering where a large group of people gather in a public place to perform a pre-planned activity. While most flash mobs are harmless, they can quickly turn into dangerous situations. They can disrupt traffic flow, cause property

Introduction to Managing Unpredictable Events: Understanding the Risks and Hazards

Unpredictable events can happen at any time and in any location. From political unrest to natural disasters, these events can cause chaos and danger for those caught in the midst of them. It is crucial to understand the risks and hazards associated with unpredictable events to manage them effectively.

This chapter will focus on the common risks and hazards associated with mobs and protests, looting, and flash mobs. Understanding these risks and hazards is essential for individuals to stay safe and avoid dangerous situations.

I. Understanding the Risks and Hazards Associated with Mobs and Protests

Mobs and protests are forms of social activism that can quickly escalate into violent and dangerous situations. These events can take place anywhere, and they often have specific triggers, such as political or social issues. While many protests are peaceful, they can turn violent without warning.

The risks and hazards associated with mobs and protests can be severe. Participants in these events may engage in violent behavior, including attacking others, damaging property, and using weapons. Tear gas, pepper spray, and rubber bullets may also be used by law enforcement to control crowds, which can cause harm to peaceful protesters.

Furthermore, outside agitators may seek to provoke violence and escalate the situation. It is also possible for bystanders to become caught in the crossfire, putting them in harm's way.

II. Understanding the Risks and Hazards Associated with Looting

Looting often occurs during periods of civil unrest, such as riots or protests. Looting involves the theft of goods from businesses, often resulting in property damage and loss of revenue. Looting can also be dangerous for individuals caught in the vicinity, as it can lead to physical altercations.

The risks and hazards associated with looting are numerous. Business owners may use force to protect their property, leading to potential physical harm. Looters may also engage in violent behavior, either towards others who are also looting or towards bystanders who may try to intervene.

Law enforcement may also be present, attempting to control the situation and prevent further looting. Tear gas and other crowd control measures may be used, leading to harm for those in the area.

III. Flash Mobs: Understanding the Dangers and Risks

Flash mobs are groups of people who gather suddenly in a public space to perform a specific action or dance. While they are often harmless and entertaining, flash mobs can be dangerous if they turn violent or if they are used as a cover for criminal activity.

The risks and hazards associated with flash mobs include the potential for violence and property damage. Participants may engage in destructive behavior, such as vandalizing property or attacking others. Flash mobs may also be used as a distraction to commit crimes, such as theft or assault.

Law enforcement may also become involved in flash mobs, attempting to control the situation and prevent violence or criminal activity. This can lead to confrontations between participants and law enforcement, potentially resulting in physical harm.

Conclusion

Understanding the risks and hazards associated with unpredictable events is essential to managing them effectively. The risks and hazards associated with mobs and protests, looting, and flash mobs can be severe, and individuals must take appropriate precautions to stay safe. In the following chapters, we will explore how to manage these risks and hazards, including assessing the situation, preparing for unpredictable events, and taking appropriate action to protect oneself and others.

Chapter 1: Assessing the Situation - Understanding the Risks and Hazards

Unpredictable events can happen at any time, and in any location, leaving individuals in danger without warning. To manage these events effectively, it is essential to understand the risks and hazards associated with them. This chapter will focus on assessing the situation to identify potential risks and hazards and the appropriate actions to take to stay safe.

I. Assessing the Situation - An Overview

Assessing the situation is the first step in managing unpredictable events. It involves understanding the risks and hazards present, evaluating one's surroundings, and deciding on an appropriate course of action. It is essential to be vigilant and aware of one's surroundings to stay safe.

II. Identifying Potential Risks and Hazards

Identifying potential risks and hazards is crucial in assessing the situation. It involves recognizing potential triggers for unpredictable events, such as political or social issues, and assessing the likelihood of these events occurring. It is important to stay informed of current events, particularly those that may have an impact on public safety.

III. Assessing One's Surroundings

Assessing one's surroundings is critical to staying safe during unpredictable events. It involves evaluating the location, such as the proximity to large crowds or potential areas of conflict, and identifying potential escape routes. It is important to avoid isolated areas or areas with limited exit points and to remain in well-lit and public areas.

IV. Understanding Crowd Behavior

Understanding crowd behavior is essential in assessing the situation during unpredictable events. It involves recognizing the dynamics of large crowds, such as the potential for crowd psychology to influence individual behavior. It is important to remain calm and avoid becoming caught up in the emotions of the crowd.

V. Preparing for Unpredictable Events

Preparing for unpredictable events is essential in managing risks and hazards. It involves having a plan in place, such as identifying a safe meeting place or means of communication in the event of an emergency. It is important to stay informed and aware of potential risks and hazards and to take steps to prepare accordingly.

VI. Taking Appropriate Action

Taking appropriate action is essential in managing risks and hazards during unpredictable events. It involves making quick and informed decisions, such as whether to evacuate the area or seek shelter. It is important to remain calm and to follow any instructions from law enforcement or emergency personnel.

VII. Staying Safe During Unpredictable Events

Staying safe during unpredictable events requires a combination of awareness, preparedness, and appropriate action. It is essential to remain vigilant, stay informed, and evaluate one's surroundings to identify potential risks and hazards. It is also important to have a plan in place, such as identifying a safe meeting place or means of communication in the event of an emergency. Taking appropriate action, such as evacuating the area or seeking shelter, is crucial to staying safe during unpredictable events.

Conclusion

Assessing the situation is the first step in managing risks and hazards during unpredictable events. It involves identifying potential risks and hazards, evaluating one's surroundings, understanding crowd behavior, preparing for unpredictable events, and taking appropriate action. By remaining vigilant, informed, and prepared, individuals can stay safe during unpredictable events. In the following chapters, we will explore specific situations, such as mobs and protests, looting, and flash mobs, and the appropriate actions to take to manage risks and hazards.

Chapter 2: Mobs and Protests - Understanding the Risks and Hazards

Mobs and protests can be powerful forms of social expression, but they can also pose significant risks and hazards to those involved or caught in the midst of them. In this chapter, we will explore the common risks and hazards associated with mobs and protests and provide guidance on how to stay safe in these situations.

I. Understanding Mobs and Protests

Mobs and protests are social expressions that involve a large gathering of people with a common goal or agenda. Mobs are typically characterized by their unpredictable behavior, while protests are often organized and peaceful. Both can involve significant numbers of people and can quickly escalate, posing risks and hazards to those involved or nearby.

II. Common Risks and Hazards Associated with Mobs and Protests

There are several common risks and hazards associated with mobs and protests, including physical harm, property damage, and the potential for violence. Mobs can quickly become dangerous, and individuals may be at risk of being trampled, assaulted, or injured. Protests can also turn violent, and police or other authorities may respond with force, including the use of tear gas or rubber bullets.

III. Preparation and Prevention

Preparation and prevention are crucial in managing the risks and hazards associated with mobs and protests. Individuals can take steps to prepare, such as remaining aware of their surroundings, identifying safe escape routes, and having a plan in place for emergencies. Prevention measures can also be taken, such as avoiding large gatherings or high-risk areas.

IV. Staying Safe During Mobs and Protests

Staying safe during mobs and protests requires a combination of preparation, awareness, and appropriate action. Individuals should remain calm and aware of their surroundings, avoiding areas where violence or conflict may occur. They should also be prepared to leave the area quickly and have a plan in place for communicating with others in the event of an emergency.

V. Dealing with Law Enforcement

During a mob or protest, individuals may come into contact with law enforcement officers, who may be present to maintain order and prevent violence. It is important to understand how to interact with law enforcement officers in these situations, including following instructions, remaining calm, and avoiding confrontations.

VI. Supporting Others

During a mob or protest, it is important to support others and provide assistance where possible. This may include helping others find safe routes to leave the area or offering assistance to those who have been injured. It is important to remain calm and act quickly in these situations.

VII. Reporting Incidents

In the event of an incident during a mob or protest, it is important to report the incident to the appropriate authorities. This may include contacting emergency services or local law enforcement. Reporting incidents can help to ensure that appropriate action is taken and that others are aware of potential risks or hazards.

Conclusion

Mobs and protests can be powerful forms of social expression, but they can also pose significant risks and hazards to those involved or caught in the midst of them. Understanding the common risks and hazards associated with mobs and protests and taking appropriate action to stay safe is essential in managing these unpredictable events. By remaining aware of their surroundings, preparing for emergencies, and taking appropriate action, individuals can stay safe during mobs and protests.

Chapter 3: Understanding the Risks and Hazards Associated with Looting

Looting can occur in a variety of settings, including natural disasters, civil unrest, and even during large-scale events. It can pose significant risks and hazards to those involved or caught in the midst of it. In this chapter, we will explore the common risks and hazards associated with looting and provide guidance on how to stay safe in these situations.

I. Understanding Looting

Looting is the act of stealing or taking goods from a property, often in the context of a larger event such as a natural disaster or civil unrest. It can be carried out by individuals or groups, and can result in significant property damage and destruction.

II. Common Risks and Hazards Associated with Looting

There are several common risks and hazards associated with looting, including physical harm, property damage, and legal consequences. Those involved in looting may face arrest or prosecution, and may be subject to violence or retaliation from others. Looting can also result in significant property damage and destruction, which can have lasting impacts on communities.

III. Preparation and Prevention

Preparation and prevention are crucial in managing the risks and hazards associated with looting. Individuals can take steps to prepare, such as securing their property and identifying safe escape routes. Prevention measures can also be taken, such as avoiding areas where looting may occur and staying informed of local news and updates.

IV. Staying Safe During Looting

Staying safe during looting requires a combination of preparation, awareness, and appropriate action. Individuals should remain calm and avoid confrontations with looters. They should also be prepared to leave the area quickly and have a plan in place for communicating with others in the event of an emergency.

V. Dealing with Law Enforcement

During an incident of looting, individuals may come into contact with law enforcement officers, who may be present to maintain order and prevent violence. It is important to understand how to interact with law enforcement officers in these situations, including following instructions, remaining calm, and avoiding confrontations.

VI. Supporting Others

During an incident of looting, it is important to support others and provide assistance where possible. This may include helping others find safe routes to leave the area or offering assistance to those who have been injured. It is important to remain calm and act quickly in these situations.

VII. Reporting Incidents

In the event of an incident of looting, it is important to report the incident to the appropriate authorities. This may include contacting emergency services or local law enforcement. Reporting incidents can help to ensure that appropriate action is taken and that others are aware of potential risks or hazards.

Conclusion

Looting can pose significant risks and hazards to those involved or caught in the midst of it. Understanding the common risks and hazards associated with looting and taking appropriate action to stay safe is essential in managing these unpredictable events. By remaining aware of their surroundings, preparing for emergencies, and taking appropriate action, individuals can stay safe during incidents of looting.

Chapter 4: Flash Mobs - Understanding the Dangers and Risks

Flash mobs are a phenomenon that has gained popularity in recent years, with groups of individuals spontaneously gathering in public places for a performance or other event. While most flash mobs are harmless and fun, they can also pose risks and hazards, especially when they are organized for other purposes, such as protests or civil unrest. In this chapter, we will explore the dangers and risks associated with flash mobs and provide guidance on how to stay safe in these situations.

I. Understanding Flash Mobs

Flash mobs are typically organized through social media or other online platforms and involve a group of individuals gathering in a public place for a coordinated performance or other event. They can occur in a variety of settings, including malls, parks, and public transportation systems.

II. Risks and Hazards of Flash Mobs

While most flash mobs are harmless, they can pose risks and hazards in certain situations. For example, flash mobs organized for protests or civil unrest can lead to violence or property damage. Flash mobs can also be used as a cover for criminal activity, such as theft or vandalism.

III. Preparation and Prevention

Preparation and prevention are crucial in managing the risks and hazards associated with flash mobs. Individuals can take steps to prepare, such as avoiding areas where flash mobs are likely to occur or identifying safe escape routes. Prevention measures can also be taken, such as staying informed of local news and updates.

IV. Staying Safe During Flash Mobs

Staying safe during flash mobs requires a combination of preparation, awareness, and appropriate action. Individuals should remain aware of their surroundings and avoid confrontations with participants in the flash mob. They should also be prepared to leave the area quickly and have a plan in place for communicating with others in the event of an emergency.

V. Dealing with Law Enforcement

During an incident involving a flash mob, individuals may come into contact with law enforcement officers, who may be present to maintain order and prevent violence. It is important to understand how to interact with law enforcement officers in these situations, including following instructions, remaining calm, and avoiding confrontations.

VI. Supporting Others

During an incident involving a flash mob, it is important to support others and provide assistance where possible. This may include helping others find safe routes to leave the area or offering assistance to those who have been injured. It is important to remain calm and act quickly in these situations.

VII. Reporting Incidents

In the event of an incident involving a flash mob, it is important to report the incident to the appropriate authorities. This may include contacting emergency services or local law enforcement. Reporting incidents can help to ensure that appropriate action is taken and that others are aware of potential risks or hazards.

Conclusion

Flash mobs can be a fun and exciting way to bring people together, but they can also pose risks and hazards in certain situations. Understanding the common risks and hazards associated with flash mobs and taking appropriate action to stay safe is essential in managing these unpredictable events. By remaining aware of their surroundings, preparing for emergencies, and taking appropriate action, individuals can stay safe during incidents involving flash mobs.

SECTION 2 PREPARING FOR THE WORST

I. Preparing for the Worst

Unpredictable events such as mobs, protests, and looting can occur at any time, anywhere, without warning. These events can pose significant risks to personal safety and property damage. To minimize the potential impact of these events, it is crucial to prepare and plan for them. This section will discuss the importance of pre-planning for managing unpredictable events, including the importance of emergency contact information, preparing an evacuation plan, and tips for staying safe during unpredictable events.

Pre-Planning for Managing Unpredictable Events

Pre-planning is a critical component of managing unpredictable events. It involves identifying potential risks and hazards, developing strategies to mitigate those risks, and having a plan in place to respond to emergencies. Pre-planning is essential for individuals, businesses, and organizations to ensure their safety and minimize the potential impact of these events.

One of the critical aspects of pre-planning is identifying and understanding the risks and hazards associated with unpredictable events. This includes the types of events that could occur, their potential impact, and the measures that can be taken to mitigate their impact. Understanding these risks and hazards can help individuals and organizations develop effective plans to manage them.

Another crucial aspect of pre-planning is establishing emergency contact information. Having updated and readily available contact information for emergency services, family, and friends is essential during unpredictable events. It is also crucial to have contact information for employees, customers, and suppliers for businesses and organizations to ensure that everyone is safe and accounted for.

Preparing an evacuation plan is also an essential component of pre-planning. An evacuation plan should include designated evacuation routes, assembly areas, and the location of emergency supplies. It should be regularly reviewed, updated, and communicated to employees, customers, and suppliers to ensure that everyone knows what to do in the event of an emergency.

In addition to pre-planning, there are several tips that individuals can follow to stay safe during unpredictable events. These include:

Staying informed: Individuals should stay informed about the event's location, status, and potential impact through reputable news sources, social media, or official alerts.

Avoiding the event: If possible, individuals should avoid the event's location to reduce the risk of injury or property damage.

Maintaining situational awareness: Individuals should remain alert and aware of their surroundings, looking out for potential risks or hazards.

Having an emergency kit: Individuals should have an emergency kit with essential supplies such as food, water, medications, and first aid kits.

Having a communication plan: Individuals should have a communication plan in place with family, friends, or colleagues to ensure that they can stay in touch during an emergency.

In conclusion, pre-planning is essential for managing unpredictable events such as mobs, protests, and looting. It involves understanding the risks and hazards associated with these events, establishing emergency contact information, preparing an evacuation plan, and following safety tips. By pre-planning for unpredictable events, individuals, businesses, and organizations can minimize their impact and ensure their safety.

Chapter 5: Pre-Planning for Managing Unpredictable Events

When it comes to managing unpredictable events, preparation is key. While it's impossible to predict every possible scenario that could occur during a protest or other public gathering, there are steps you can take to be better prepared to handle any situation that arises. In this chapter, we'll discuss pre-planning tips that can help you stay safe during unpredictable events.

Stay Informed

The first step to preparing for unpredictable events is to stay informed. This means keeping up to date with news and information about the event or protest you plan to attend. You can do this by monitoring social media accounts, following local news outlets, and subscribing to emergency alerts.

Additionally, it's important to research the laws and regulations regarding protests and public gatherings in your area. Familiarize yourself with the local laws and regulations so that you can be better prepared to handle any potential legal issues that may arise.

Develop a Communication Plan

In an unpredictable event, communication is critical. Having a plan in place can help you stay in touch with loved ones and ensure that everyone is accounted for. Consider developing a communication plan that includes the following:

Emergency contact information: Make a list of emergency contacts, including the names and phone numbers of at least three people you trust, such as family members, friends, or coworkers.

Meeting points: Establish a designated meeting point in case you get separated from your group.

Communication methods: Determine how you will communicate with your group, whether it be via text message, social media, or other means.

Establish a check-in system: Set up a system for checking in with each other periodically throughout the event.

Plan Your Exit Strategy

Before attending any unpredictable event, it's important to plan your exit strategy. This means identifying multiple exit routes and having a plan in place for how you will leave the area in case of an emergency. Some tips for planning your exit strategy include:

Identify multiple exit routes: Familiarize yourself with the layout of the area and identify at least two or three potential exit routes.

Avoid bottlenecks: Try to avoid areas where large groups of people are funneling through narrow exits or corridors.

Consider alternative modes of transportation: If possible, consider alternative modes of transportation, such as bikes or scooters, that can help you quickly leave the area if needed.

Have a backup plan: In case your primary exit route is blocked or otherwise unavailable, have a backup plan in place.

Prepare an Emergency Kit

In an unpredictable event, it's important to be self-sufficient for at least a short period of time. Consider preparing an emergency kit that includes the following:

First aid kit: Include bandages, antiseptic wipes, gauze, and other basic first aid supplies.

Water and non-perishable snacks: Pack at least one gallon of water per person, as well as non-perishable snacks that can sustain you for several hours.

Portable phone charger: Make sure you have a portable phone charger or extra batteries for your phone.

Cash: In case of an emergency, it's always a good idea to have some cash on hand.

Dress Appropriately

When attending an unpredictable event, it's important to dress appropriately for the weather and the potential risks of the event. Here are some tips for dressing appropriately:

Wear comfortable shoes: You may be on your feet for hours, so make sure to wear comfortable shoes that you can walk in for extended periods of time.

Dress in layers: Depending on the weather and the potential risks of the event, you may need to dress in layers

Chapter 6: The Importance of Emergency Contact Information

In times of unpredictable events, having access to reliable emergency contact information is crucial. Knowing who to call and how to reach them can help you and those around you stay safe and secure. In this chapter, we will discuss the importance of having emergency contact information readily available and tips on how to ensure that you have the right information at your fingertips.

Understanding the Importance of Emergency Contact Information

Emergency contact information includes the names, phone numbers, and other relevant details of individuals who can be contacted in the event of an emergency. This information is critical because it provides responders with a way to contact your loved ones and inform them of your situation in case you are unable to do so yourself.

Having accurate and up-to-date emergency contact information is particularly important for those who live alone or have special medical needs. In case of an emergency, first responders need to know if there are any special instructions or health concerns they should be aware of. Additionally, if you are in a situation where you are unable to speak, emergency responders need to know whom to contact on your behalf.

Incorporating Emergency Contact Information into Your Everyday Life

To ensure that your emergency contact information is readily available when needed, it's important to incorporate it into your everyday life. Here are some ways to make sure that you always have access to this crucial information:

Store Your Emergency Contact Information in Your Phone

Most smartphones have a built-in feature that allows you to store emergency contact information that can be accessed even when your phone is locked. Take the time to input your emergency contacts into your phone's contacts list and label them as such. This way, first responders will be able to quickly and easily access this information.

Carry an Emergency Contact Card

In addition to storing emergency contact information in your phone, it's a good idea to carry an emergency contact card with you at all times. This card should include your name, emergency contacts, and any relevant medical information. You can create your own emergency contact card or purchase one online.

Share Your Emergency Contact Information with Friends and Family

Make sure that your emergency contacts are aware that they are your designated contacts and provide them with any relevant information they may need. Additionally, share your emergency contact information with friends and family members who live nearby or may need to contact your emergency contacts in case of an emergency.

Keep Your Emergency Contact Information Updated

Review your emergency contact information regularly and update it as needed. Make sure that your designated contacts are still willing and able to serve in this role, and update any medical information or instructions as needed.

Conclusion

Emergency contact information is a vital component of any emergency preparedness plan. By taking the time to ensure that you have accurate and up-to-date emergency contact information readily available, you can help ensure that you and those around you stay safe in the event of an emergency. Incorporate these tips into your everyday life to ensure that you always have access to this critical information.

Chapter 7: Preparing an Evacuation Plan

In times of unpredictable events such as mobs, protests, and looting, it's essential to be prepared for the worst-case scenario. One important aspect of preparation is having a solid evacuation plan in place. This chapter will discuss the steps you can take to prepare an effective evacuation plan to ensure your safety in the event of an emergency.

Step 1: Identify Potential Evacuation Routes

The first step in preparing an evacuation plan is to identify potential evacuation routes. You should have at least two escape routes planned out in case one becomes blocked or unsafe. Consider both primary and alternative routes, and take into account any obstacles that may prevent you from using a particular route.

It's also important to know the location of emergency exits in buildings, particularly in public spaces like shopping malls, cinemas, and sports arenas. Familiarize yourself with the nearest exits and how to quickly reach them. Be aware of any locked or obstructed exits, and report them to the appropriate authorities if necessary.

Step 2: Create a Communication Plan

Communication is key in any emergency situation. You should establish a communication plan with your family or group to ensure that everyone knows what to do and where to go in case of an emergency. Make sure everyone has each other's contact information, including phone numbers and email addresses, and establish a meeting point where you can regroup.

If you have children or elderly family members, make sure they know the evacuation plan and what to do in case they become separated from you. Designate a specific person to be responsible for their safety and make sure they have their contact information.

Step 3: Prepare an Emergency Kit

In the event of an emergency evacuation, you may not have time to gather necessary items. It's essential to prepare an emergency kit ahead of time that contains items such as food, water, first aid supplies, and any necessary medications.

Your emergency kit should also include important documents such as identification cards, insurance policies, and copies of important medical records. Consider storing these items in a waterproof container or bag to protect them from damage.

Step 4: Practice Your Evacuation Plan

Once you have created an evacuation plan, it's important to practice it regularly. Conducting drills can help ensure that everyone knows what to do in case of an emergency and can help identify any potential issues with your plan.

During your practice drills, pay attention to the amount of time it takes to evacuate and any areas that may cause congestion or confusion. Make adjustments to your plan as needed to ensure that everyone can evacuate safely and quickly.

Step 5: Stay Informed

Finally, staying informed is crucial during an emergency. Monitor local news and social media channels for updates and information about the situation. Follow the instructions of emergency personnel and be prepared to adjust your evacuation plan if necessary.

Conclusion

Preparing an effective evacuation plan is a critical component of managing unpredictable events. By identifying potential evacuation routes, creating a communication plan, preparing an emergency kit, practicing your evacuation plan, and staying informed, you can help ensure your safety in the event of an emergency. Remember to always prioritize your safety and the safety of those around you.

Chapter 8: Tips for Staying Safe During Unpredictable Events

Unpredictable events can happen at any time, and it's important to be prepared for them. Whether it's a protest, a flash mob, or a natural disaster, there are steps you can take to increase your safety and decrease your chances of harm. In this chapter, we will discuss some tips for staying safe during unpredictable events.

Stay Informed

One of the most important things you can do to stay safe during an unpredictable event is to stay informed. Pay attention to news and social media updates, as they can provide valuable information about what is happening and where. Make sure you have access to a reliable source of information, and keep your phone charged so that you can receive updates.

Plan Ahead

Before attending an event, make a plan with friends or family members. Agree on a meeting place in case you get separated, and make sure everyone knows how to get there. If you're driving, plan your route in advance and avoid areas that are likely to be affected by the event.

Dress Appropriately

Wearing appropriate clothing can make a big difference in your safety during unpredictable events. Avoid wearing anything that could be considered provocative or offensive, as it could make you a target. Wear comfortable shoes that you can run in if necessary, and consider dressing in layers so that you can adjust to changing weather conditions.

Carry Identification and Emergency Contact Information

Carry identification with you at all times, and make sure that your emergency contact information is up-to-date. If you have a medical condition, consider wearing a medical alert bracelet or necklace. Keep a list of emergency contacts in your phone or wallet, and make sure that your loved ones have your contact information as well.

Stay Calm

During unpredictable events, it's important to stay calm. Panic can make situations worse, and it can increase your chances of harm. Take deep breaths and try to focus on your surroundings. If you feel overwhelmed, find a quiet place to take a break and regroup.

Stay Alert

Keep an eye on your surroundings and be aware of potential danger. Avoid getting too close to the action, and stay away from areas where violence or looting is likely to occur. If you see something suspicious, report it to law enforcement immediately.

Trust Your Gut

If something doesn't feel right, trust your instincts. Don't be afraid to leave an event if you feel uncomfortable or unsafe. If you feel that you're in danger, call 911 or seek help from law enforcement or other emergency personnel.

Have a Plan for Evacuation

If the situation becomes dangerous, have a plan for evacuation. Identify possible escape routes in advance and make sure that everyone in your group knows where they are. If possible, avoid using elevators and take the stairs instead. Remember to stay calm and move quickly, but don't run unless absolutely necessary.

Stay Connected

Stay connected with friends and family members throughout the event. Use text messaging or social media to stay in touch, and let them know that you're safe. If you get separated, make sure that everyone knows where to meet up afterwards.

Take Care of Yourself Afterwards

After the event is over, take care of yourself both physically and mentally. Get plenty of rest, eat nutritious food, and seek help if you're experiencing any emotional distress. Talk to friends and family members about your experience, and consider seeking professional counseling if necessary.

In conclusion, unpredictable events can be scary and dangerous, but there are steps you can take to increase your safety and reduce your risk of harm. By staying informed, planning ahead, dressing appropriately, carrying identification and emergency contact information,

SECTION 3   STRATEGIES FOR STAYING SAFE

INTRODUCTION

Section III: Strategies for Staying Safe

Unpredictable events, such as mobs, protests, looting, and flash mobs, can be dangerous and stressful experiences. While it is impossible to completely eliminate the risks associated with these situations, there are steps that individuals can take to increase their safety and protect themselves from harm. In this section, we will explore some practical strategies for staying safe during these events.

Chapter 9 will focus specifically on strategies for staying safe during mobs and protests. We will discuss how to prepare for these events, how to avoid potential hazards, and what to do if you find yourself caught in the middle of a protest or mob. Chapter 10 will cover tips for protecting yourself during a looting event, including how to avoid becoming a target, how to secure your property, and what to do if you witness a looting incident.

In Chapter 11, we will examine strategies for staying safe during flash mobs. While flash mobs are often harmless and fun events, they can also become chaotic and dangerous if they are not properly managed. We will discuss how to identify and avoid potential dangers, as well as what to do if you find yourself caught up in a flash mob.

Finally, Chapter 12 will emphasize the importance of staying informed during unpredictable events. We will explore various sources of information, including social media, news outlets, and emergency alerts, and provide tips for accessing accurate and timely information. By staying informed, you can make informed decisions about your safety and take appropriate actions to protect yourself and those around you.

Throughout this section, we will emphasize the importance of remaining calm and vigilant, trusting your instincts, and taking proactive measures to stay safe during unpredictable events. By preparing yourself and following the strategies outlined in this section, you can increase your chances of staying safe and avoiding harm during these events.

Chapter 9: Strategies for Staying Safe During Mobs and Protests

Mobs and protests can be unpredictable, and the potential for violence and danger is high. It is essential to have a plan and take precautions to stay safe during these events. In this chapter, we will discuss some strategies for staying safe during mobs and protests.

Educate Yourself on the Event

The first step in staying safe during a protest is to educate yourself on the event. Research the organization that is hosting the protest, the reason for the protest, and any potential counter-protests. Understanding the goals and motivations of the organizers and other attendees can help you anticipate potential risks and stay safe.

Plan Your Route

When attending a protest, plan your route in advance. Avoid large crowds and keep to the edges of the protest to minimize your risk of being caught in a violent confrontation. Familiarize yourself with the area, so you know where the nearest exits and safe locations are.

Dress Appropriately

Your attire can impact your safety during a protest. Avoid wearing clothing that identifies you as a supporter of a particular group or cause. Dress in layers, so you can adjust your clothing based on the weather and the intensity of the protest. Wear comfortable shoes that you can run in if necessary.

Stay Alert

During a protest, stay alert and aware of your surroundings. Avoid using your phone or other electronic devices that may distract you. Keep an eye out for potential threats, such as aggressive protesters or law enforcement officers. Be prepared to move quickly if necessary.

Stay Calm

Protests can be emotional and intense, but it's essential to remain calm. Avoid engaging in confrontations with protesters or law enforcement officers, as this can escalate the situation quickly. If you feel yourself getting overwhelmed or anxious, take a break and step away from the protest.

Have a Communication Plan

Before attending a protest, establish a communication plan with friends or family members. Determine a meeting place in case you get separated or have to evacuate the area quickly. Make sure everyone in your group has each other's contact information and establish a method of communication, such as texting or calling.

Know Your Rights

As a participant in a protest, it's essential to know your rights. Review your rights to free speech and assembly, and familiarize yourself with any local laws or regulations that may apply. If you believe your rights are being violated, seek legal advice or contact the American Civil Liberties Union (ACLU) or other legal organizations for assistance.

Seek Medical Assistance if Necessary

If you are injured during a protest, seek medical assistance immediately. Carry a basic first aid kit with you, and familiarize yourself with the location of nearby medical facilities. If you witness someone else being injured, call for medical assistance or seek help from law enforcement officers.

Document the Event

Documenting the event can provide valuable information for legal or advocacy purposes. Record any incidents of violence or harassment, and take photos or videos if possible. Be sure to respect the privacy of other protesters and avoid taking photos or videos of them without their consent.

Practice Self-Care

After attending a protest, it's essential to practice self-care. Participating in protests can be emotionally and physically exhausting, so take time to rest and recuperate. Engage in activities that make you feel calm and centered, such as meditation or yoga.

Conclusion:

Participating in a protest can be a powerful way to make your voice heard, but it's essential to prioritize your safety. By following these strategies, you can reduce your risk of injury and stay safe during a protest. Remember to stay informed, stay alert, and stay calm.

Chapter 10: The Importance of Staying Informed During Unpredictable Events

In unpredictable events such as mobs, protests, looting, and flash mobs, staying informed is crucial to staying safe. It is important to know what is happening in your immediate surroundings, as well as in the larger context of the event. This chapter will provide tips and strategies for staying informed during unpredictable events.

Keep an Eye on the News

One of the best ways to stay informed during unpredictable events is to keep an eye on the news. This can be done through various sources such as television news channels, news websites, social media, and radio. It is important to follow reliable sources of news and avoid spreading rumors or unverified information.

Use Social Media Wisely

Social media can be a valuable tool for staying informed during unpredictable events. However, it is important to use it wisely and with caution. Social media platforms such as Twitter, Facebook, and Instagram can provide real-time updates from eyewitnesses and reporters on the ground. It is important to follow reliable sources and use hashtags to filter relevant information.

Listen to Emergency Broadcasts

During unpredictable events, emergency broadcasts may be used to provide important information to the public. These broadcasts can be heard on radio and television, and can provide information such as evacuation orders, curfew information, and safety tips.

Sign Up for Emergency Alerts

Many cities and municipalities have emergency alert systems that can send text messages, emails, or phone calls to residents in case of an emergency. These alerts can provide information such as evacuation orders, shelter-in-place orders, and other important information.

Use Mobile Apps

There are various mobile apps that can be used to stay informed during unpredictable events. These apps can provide real-time updates on the situation, maps of the affected areas, and safety tips. Some popular apps include Citizen, Nextdoor, and Emergency.

Stay Alert and Aware of Your Surroundings

While it is important to stay informed through various sources, it is also important to stay alert and aware of your surroundings. Pay attention to any signs of danger or potential threats, and be ready to take action if necessary. Keep an eye out for any suspicious behavior or objects, and report them to the authorities if needed.

Have a Communication Plan

In case of an emergency, it is important to have a communication plan with your family, friends, or coworkers. This plan should include designated meeting points, contact information, and emergency procedures. Make sure everyone in your group is aware of the plan and knows what to do in case of an emergency.

Use Common Sense

Lastly, it is important to use common sense and good judgment during unpredictable events. Avoid unnecessary risks, and stay away from areas that may be dangerous or crowded. Follow the instructions of law enforcement officials, and avoid confrontations with protesters or other individuals.

In conclusion, staying informed during unpredictable events is crucial to staying safe. Use various sources of information such as news, social media, emergency broadcasts, and mobile apps to stay up-to-date on the situation. Stay alert and aware of your surroundings, and have a communication plan with your family, friends, or coworkers. By using common sense and good judgment, you can increase your chances of staying safe during unpredictable events.

Having reliable information can help you make that decision based on the risks involved.

Finally, staying informed can help you prepare for unpredictable events. For example, if you know that a hurricane is approaching your area, you can take measures to prepare your home and evacuate if necessary.

How to Obtain Reliable Information

Obtaining reliable information during unpredictable events can be challenging, as misinformation and rumors can spread quickly. However, there are several ways to obtain reliable information:

Local News Sources: Local news sources such as newspapers, TV stations, and radio stations often provide up-to-date information on unpredictable events in your area. It is important to choose reputable news sources that have a track record of providing reliable information.

Social Media: Social media platforms such as Twitter, Facebook, and Instagram can be a useful source of information during unpredictable events. However, it is important to be cautious when using social media as rumors and misinformation can spread quickly.

Emergency Alerts: Many local and state governments have emergency alert systems in place that provide up-to-date information on unpredictable events. These alerts can be delivered via text message, email, or phone call.

Mobile Apps: There are several mobile apps available that provide up-to-date information on unpredictable events. Examples include the Red Cross Emergency App and the FEMA app.

Using Information to Stay Safe

Obtaining reliable information is only the first step in staying safe during unpredictable events. You also need to know how to use that information to stay safe. Here are some tips:

Plan Ahead: Before an unpredictable event occurs, develop a plan for staying safe. For example, identify safe locations where you can seek shelter or evacuation routes in case of a natural disaster.

Stay Alert: Pay attention to your surroundings and be aware of potential dangers. If you notice anything suspicious, report it to authorities immediately.

Follow Authorities' Instructions: During unpredictable events, local authorities may issue instructions or warnings. It is important to follow these instructions to stay safe.

Use Common Sense: Use common sense when making decisions about your safety. For example, if an area looks unsafe, avoid it.

Stay Calm: During unpredictable events, it is important to stay calm and avoid panic. Panic can lead to poor decision-making and increase the risk of injury.

Conclusion

Staying informed is critical for staying safe during unpredictable events. Obtaining reliable information and knowing how to use that information to stay safe can help you make informed decisions about your safety and avoid potentially dangerous situations. By planning ahead, staying alert, following authorities' instructions, using common sense, and staying calm

This cannot be over stressed enough.

Chapter 11: Tips for Protecting Yourself During a Looting Event.

Looting can be a dangerous and unpredictable event, with looters often resorting to violence and destruction of property. It's important to know how to protect yourself in such situations to ensure your safety. In this chapter, we'll discuss some tips for protecting yourself during a looting event.

Avoid the Area

The best way to protect yourself during a looting event is to avoid the area altogether. If you hear that there is a potential looting event happening nearby, stay away from the area and find a safe place to wait it out. If you're already in the area when the looting begins, try to leave as quickly and safely as possible.

Stay Inside

If you can't avoid the area, the next best thing is to stay inside a building. Find a secure room with a lockable door and stay there until the situation calms down. Make sure to keep any windows or doors locked and stay away from them.

Stay Alert

If you can't avoid the area and can't stay inside, stay alert and aware of your surroundings. Keep an eye on the crowd and try to stay on the outskirts of it. Be prepared to leave quickly if the situation escalates.

Don't Engage

It's important to remember not to engage with the looters. Don't try to confront them or reason with them, as this can escalate the situation and put you in danger. Keep a low profile and try to blend in with the crowd to avoid drawing attention to yourself.

Have an Exit Plan

If you do find yourself in the middle of a looting event, make sure you have an exit plan. Know where the exits are and be prepared to leave quickly if necessary. Try to stay close to the exits and avoid getting trapped in a crowd.

Stay Calm

In any unpredictable event, it's important to stay calm. Don't panic or make sudden movements that could attract attention to yourself. Stay quiet and don't draw attention to yourself.

Call for Help

If you're in immediate danger, call for help. Call the police or emergency services and give them as much information as possible about your location and the situation. If you're unable to make a call, try to send a text message or use social media to alert someone to your situation.

Follow Authorities' Instructions

If the police or other authorities arrive on the scene, follow their instructions. They are there to help and keep you safe. If they tell you to leave, do so quickly and calmly.

In conclusion, looting events can be dangerous and unpredictable, but by following these tips, you can protect yourself and stay safe. Remember to stay alert, have an exit plan, and call for help if you're in immediate danger. Stay calm and follow the authorities' instructions to ensure your safety.

Chapter 12: Strategies for Staying Safe During Flash Mobs

Flash mobs are typically organized through social media and involve a large group of people gathering at a specific location to perform a prearranged activity. While most flash mobs are harmless and fun, some can turn violent and pose a threat to public safety. In this chapter, we will discuss strategies for staying safe during flash mobs.

Be Aware of Your Surroundings

The first and most important strategy for staying safe during flash mobs is to be aware of your surroundings. Pay attention to the people around you and any unusual activity. If you notice anything suspicious or threatening, leave the area immediately.

Avoid Flash Mob Areas

If you know that a flash mob is planned for a specific location, it is best to avoid that area altogether. If you cannot avoid the area, make sure you have a plan in place for what to do if the situation turns violent.

Travel in Groups

It is always safer to travel in groups, especially when attending events that attract large crowds. Stick together with your friends or family members, and make sure everyone knows where the others are at all times.

Stay on the Periphery

If you do decide to attend a flash mob, it is best to stay on the periphery of the crowd. Avoid being in the center of the action, where things can quickly get out of control.

Dress Appropriately

Make sure to dress appropriately for the event. Avoid wearing clothing or accessories that could make you a target or that could get caught on something.

Carry a Phone and ID

Always carry your phone and identification with you. Make sure your phone is fully charged, and keep it easily accessible in case of an emergency.

Have an Escape Plan

It is important to have an escape plan in case things turn violent. Identify escape routes ahead of time, and make sure everyone in your group knows where to meet if you get separated.

Follow the Instructions of Law Enforcement

If law enforcement is present, follow their instructions. They are there to help keep everyone safe, and it is important to cooperate with them.

Stay Calm

If you find yourself caught in the middle of a flash mob that turns violent, try to stay calm. Do not panic or become aggressive, as this can escalate the situation. Instead, look for a way to safely exit the area.

Report Suspicious Activity

If you notice any suspicious activity or behavior, report it to law enforcement immediately. This can help prevent a dangerous situation from escalating.

Conclusion

Attending a flash mob can be a fun and exciting experience, but it is important to be aware of the potential risks and to take steps to stay safe. By following these strategies, you can minimize the risk of becoming a victim of violence or other dangerous situations during a flash mob event. Remember to always be aware of your surroundings, travel in groups, and have a plan in place for what to do in case of an emergency.

If you find yourself caught up in a mob, riot, or protest, it's important to remain calm and think clearly in order to stay safe. Depending on the situation, there are different strategies that can be employed to protect yourself and avoid harm.

Assess the Situation

The first step when finding yourself in the middle of a mob, riot, or protest is to assess the situation. Is the crowd peaceful or violent? Is there a police presence? Are people agitated and emotional, or are they calm and collected? Taking stock of these factors will help you determine the appropriate course of action.

Stay Calm

It's natural to feel scared and anxious when surrounded by a large group of people who are behaving in a potentially dangerous manner. However, it's important to try to remain calm and composed. Panicking can cause you to make poor decisions that could put you in harm's way.

Move to the Perimeter

If possible, try to move to the outer edge of the crowd. This will give you more space and help you avoid getting caught up in the middle of the action. Keep your distance from the crowd and try to move along the edge of the protest or riot.

Avoid Confrontation

It's important to avoid confrontation with other individuals in the crowd. If someone is behaving aggressively, try to move away from them. Don't engage in verbal or physical altercations, as this can escalate the situation and put you in danger.

Stick with a Group

If you're with a group of people, stick together. This can provide you with some sense of security and make it easier to navigate through the crowd. Make sure to establish a meeting point in case you get separated.

Follow Police Instructions

If there is a police presence, listen carefully to their instructions. They may tell you to disperse or move to a specific location. It's important to follow these instructions in order to avoid getting caught in the middle of a dangerous situation.

Protect Your Head

If violence breaks out, it's important to protect your head. Use your arms to shield your head and neck from blows. If you're wearing a backpack or bag, use it to cushion your head.

Seek Shelter

If the situation becomes too dangerous, seek shelter in a nearby building or store. Lock the doors and stay away from windows until the situation has calmed down.

Stay Informed

Stay informed about the situation by checking news sources and social media. This can help you determine if it's safe to leave your location or if you should wait until the situation has been resolved.

Seek Medical Attention

If you are injured during a protest or riot, seek medical attention as soon as possible. Even minor injuries can become serious if left untreated.

In summary, if you find yourself caught up in a mob, riot, or protest, stay calm, move to the perimeter, avoid confrontation, stick with a group, follow police instructions, protect your head, seek shelter, stay informed, and seek medical attention if necessary. By taking these steps, you can increase your chances of staying safe during unpredictable events.

SECTION 4   AFTERMATH AND RECOVERY

INTRODUCTION

Section IV: Aftermath and Recovery

In the aftermath of an unpredictable event, the road to recovery can be long and arduous. Whether you have experienced a mob riot, protest, or looting event, the aftermath can be overwhelming and difficult to navigate. It is crucial to be prepared for the aftermath and have a plan in place to cope with the aftermath and recover as quickly as possible.

Chapter 13: The Importance of Being Prepared for the Aftermath

Preparing for the aftermath of an unpredictable event is just as important as preparing for the event itself. Being prepared can help you cope with the aftermath and recover more quickly. In this chapter, we will discuss the importance of being prepared for the aftermath and provide tips on how to prepare.

Chapter 14: Dealing with the Aftermath of Mobs and Protests

The aftermath of a mob riot or protest can be chaotic and unpredictable. There may be damage to property and infrastructure, injuries or fatalities, and emotional trauma. It is essential to have a plan in place to deal with the aftermath and start the recovery process as quickly as possible. This chapter will provide tips on how to deal with the aftermath of mobs and protests, including how to assess damage and work with law enforcement and local officials.

Chapter 15: Recovering After a Looting Event

If you have experienced a looting event, the aftermath can be devastating. You may have lost valuable property, and your sense of security may be shattered. Recovering from a looting event takes time and effort, but it is possible. In this chapter, we will discuss how to start the recovery process after a looting event, including steps to take to assess damage, work with insurance companies, and restore your sense of security.

Chapter 16: Coping with the Aftermath of Flash Mobs

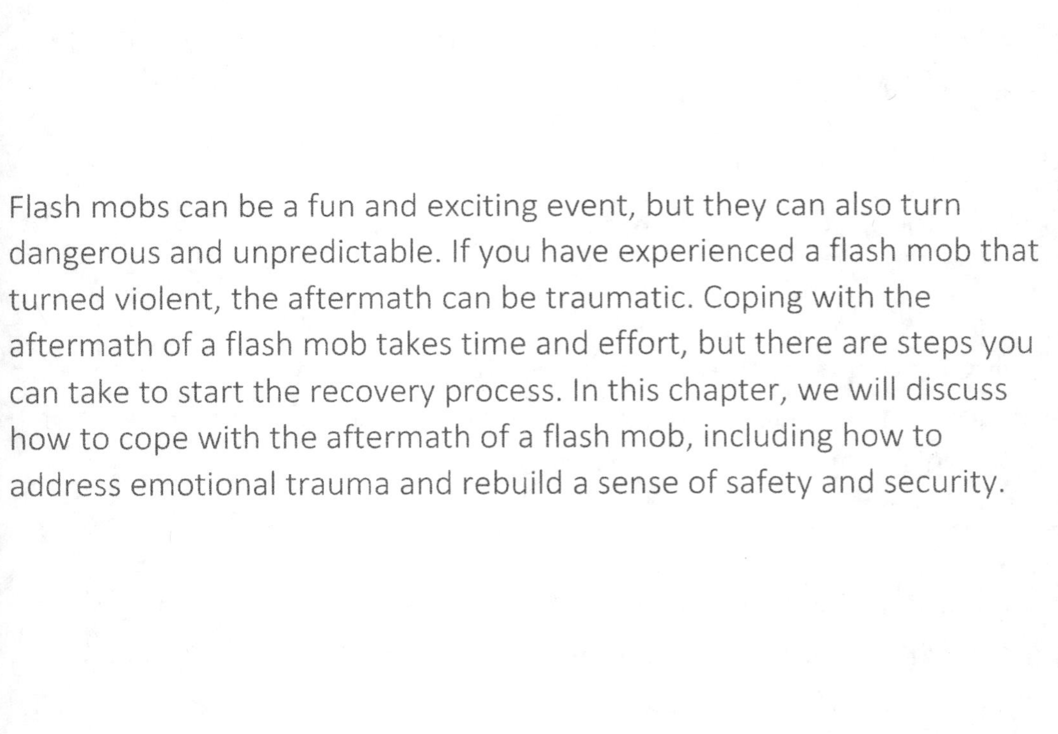

Flash mobs can be a fun and exciting event, but they can also turn dangerous and unpredictable. If you have experienced a flash mob that turned violent, the aftermath can be traumatic. Coping with the aftermath of a flash mob takes time and effort, but there are steps you can take to start the recovery process. In this chapter, we will discuss how to cope with the aftermath of a flash mob, including how to address emotional trauma and rebuild a sense of safety and security.

Chapter 13: The Importance of Being Prepared for the Aftermath

In any unpredictable event, whether it be a mob riot or a natural disaster, being prepared for the aftermath is just as important as being prepared for the event itself. Aftermath and recovery can be a difficult and challenging time, and without proper preparation, it can become even more overwhelming. This chapter will discuss the importance of being prepared for the aftermath of unpredictable events and provide tips on how to do so.

Why is it Important to be Prepared for the Aftermath?

Being prepared for the aftermath of an unpredictable event can help to minimize the impact of the event and aid in recovery. Preparation can help individuals and communities to:

Minimize physical and emotional harm: After an unpredictable event, individuals may be exposed to physical and emotional harm, such as injuries, trauma, and stress. Being prepared can help to minimize these risks and help individuals to recover more quickly.

Ensure basic needs are met: An unpredictable event can disrupt basic services such as electricity, water, and food. Being prepared can help individuals to ensure that their basic needs are met, even if services are disrupted.

Aid in the recovery process: The aftermath of an unpredictable event can be a difficult and challenging time. Being prepared can help to aid in the recovery process and help individuals and communities to rebuild.

Tips for Being Prepared for the Aftermath

Have a plan: Create a plan for what to do in the aftermath of an unpredictable event. This plan should include information on how to contact loved ones, where to go for assistance, and how to access basic needs such as food and water.

Stock up on supplies: Stock up on supplies such as food, water, and medication. These supplies should be sufficient for at least three days.

Stay informed: Stay informed about the situation by listening to local news and following official social media accounts. This can help individuals to stay up-to-date on the situation and any new developments.

Seek help if needed: After an unpredictable event, it is common to experience physical and emotional distress. If needed, seek help from professionals such as doctors, counselors, or therapists.

Connect with community resources: Connect with community resources such as local government, nonprofit organizations, and community centers. These resources can provide valuable information and assistance during the aftermath and recovery process.

Conclusion

Being prepared for the aftermath of an unpredictable event is essential to minimizing harm and aiding in recovery. By having a plan, stocking up on supplies, staying informed, seeking help if needed, and connecting with community resources, individuals and communities can be better equipped to deal with the aftermath of an unpredictable event.

Chapter 14: Dealing with the Aftermath of Mobs and Protests

Mobs and protests are unpredictable events that can turn violent and destructive, leaving behind a trail of damage and chaos. Dealing with the aftermath of these events can be overwhelming and stressful, especially for those who have been directly affected. In this chapter, we will discuss strategies for coping with the aftermath of mobs and protests.

Ensure Your Safety: The first step in dealing with the aftermath of a mob or protest is to ensure your safety. If you have been caught up in the event, make sure to seek medical attention if needed and report any injuries to the authorities. If you are still in the area, stay away from any remaining crowds and seek shelter in a safe location.

Assess the Damage: Once you are in a safe location, assess the damage that has been done. If your property has been damaged or destroyed, document the damage by taking photos or videos. This evidence will be helpful when filing insurance claims or seeking assistance from the government.

Contact Your Insurance Provider: If you have insurance coverage for damage caused by riots, looting, or civil unrest, contact your insurance provider as soon as possible. They will guide you through the claims process and provide you with information on what is covered under your policy.

File a Police Report: It is important to file a police report as soon as possible, even if the damage is minor. This report will provide a record of the event and may be required by your insurance provider or the government when seeking assistance.

Seek Assistance: Depending on the severity of the damage, you may need to seek assistance from the government or community organizations. Contact your local government officials or community organizations to find out what assistance is available in your area.

Take Care of Yourself: Dealing with the aftermath of a mob or protest can be emotionally and physically draining. It is important to take care of yourself during this time. Make sure to eat well, get enough rest, and seek support from family, friends, or a mental health professional if needed.

Rebuilding and Moving Forward: Once the immediate aftermath has been addressed, it is time to start rebuilding and moving forward. This may involve repairing or rebuilding your property, replacing lost items, and finding ways to prevent future damage.

Dealing with the aftermath of a mob or protest can be a challenging experience, but with the right strategies in place, it is possible to recover and move forward. Remember to prioritize your safety and well-being, seek assistance when needed, and take the necessary steps to rebuild and move forward.

Chapter 15: Recovering After a Looting Event

Looting events can be traumatic and can leave individuals feeling violated and vulnerable. In the aftermath of a looting event, it is important to take steps towards recovery and healing. This chapter will provide guidance on how to recover after a looting event, including practical and emotional strategies.

Secure Your Property and Assess the Damage

The first step towards recovery after a looting event is to secure your property and assess the damage. It is important to document any damage that has been done and to take pictures of the areas that have been affected. This documentation will be helpful when filing an insurance claim or seeking assistance from local authorities.

If possible, make any necessary repairs or take steps to secure the property to prevent further damage or theft. Consider installing security cameras, reinforcing doors and windows, or adding additional locks to deter future break-ins.

Contact Your Insurance Company

Contact your insurance company as soon as possible to report the looting event and begin the claims process. Be prepared to provide documentation of the damage, including photographs and a detailed list of any stolen items.

Your insurance company can provide guidance on how to proceed with the claims process and what documentation is needed. They may also be able to provide information on any additional resources or support available to you.

Seek Emotional Support

Experiencing a looting event can be traumatic and can leave individuals feeling anxious, scared, and vulnerable. It is important to seek emotional support during this time.

Consider reaching out to friends or family for support, or seeking the help of a mental health professional. Talking about the experience with a therapist can be helpful in processing the trauma and developing coping strategies.

There are also support groups and resources available for those who have experienced a similar event. Local community organizations or religious groups may provide support or resources to those in need.

Develop a Plan for Moving Forward

After a looting event, it can be difficult to know how to move forward. Developing a plan for moving forward can be helpful in regaining a sense of control and creating a path towards recovery.

Consider setting small, achievable goals for yourself, such as repairing or replacing damaged items, or taking steps to increase security measures. Focus on rebuilding a sense of safety and security in your home or business.

It may also be helpful to seek the advice of a financial advisor or accountant, particularly if there has been financial loss as a result of the looting event. They can provide guidance on how to recover financially and create a plan for moving forward.

Take Care of Yourself

During the recovery process, it is important to prioritize self-care. This may include engaging in activities that bring you joy or provide a sense of relaxation, such as exercise, meditation, or spending time in nature.

Take care of your physical health by eating well, getting enough sleep, and seeking medical attention if necessary. It is also important to stay connected with friends and loved ones and to seek support when needed.

Consider Legal Action

In some cases, it may be appropriate to consider legal action after a looting event. If the event was the result of criminal activity, it is important to report it to the authorities and cooperate with any investigations.

Legal action may also be appropriate if there was negligence on the part of property owners or security personnel. Consider consulting with a lawyer to explore your legal options.

In conclusion, recovering after a looting event can be a difficult and challenging process. It is important to take steps towards healing and regaining a sense of safety and security. Seeking emotional support, developing a plan for moving forward, and prioritizing self-care can all be helpful strategies in the recovery process.

Chapter 16: Coping with the Aftermath of Flash Mobs

Flash mobs are a phenomenon that has been around for several years now. It's an organized gathering of people, who assemble at a predetermined location and carry out a performance or activity for a short time before dispersing. While most flash mobs are harmless and meant to bring joy, some have been known to turn violent and cause destruction.

If you've been caught up in a flash mob event that has turned violent, the aftermath can be traumatic and overwhelming. Coping with the aftermath of a flash mob requires a different approach than other unpredictable events, as the damage caused is often immediate and can have long-lasting effects.

Recognize the Impact of the Event

The first step in coping with the aftermath of a flash mob is to recognize the impact of the event on your mental and emotional well-being. Being caught up in a violent flash mob can cause fear, anxiety, and a sense of helplessness. It's important to acknowledge these feelings and understand that they are a normal reaction to a traumatic event.

Seek Support

After experiencing a traumatic event like a violent flash mob, it's essential to seek support from family, friends, or professionals. Don't isolate yourself; instead, reach out to someone you trust and talk about your experience. If your feelings are overwhelming, it may be helpful to speak with a therapist or counselor who can provide you with coping strategies and support.

Take Care of Yourself

Taking care of yourself physically and mentally is crucial in coping with the aftermath of a flash mob. Ensure that you get enough rest, eat healthily, and exercise regularly. Avoid using drugs or alcohol to cope with your feelings, as this can worsen the situation. Engage in activities that make you feel good, such as spending time with loved ones, listening to music, or engaging in a hobby.

Understand Your Rights

It's essential to understand your rights if you've been a victim of a violent flash mob. If you've been injured or experienced property damage, you may be eligible for compensation or assistance. Contact a lawyer or seek advice from legal aid organizations to understand your options.

Document the Event

Documenting the event can be helpful in processing your experience and seeking justice. If possible, take photographs or videos of the event and any damage caused. Write down your account of what happened, including the date, time, and location of the flash mob. This information can be helpful in providing evidence if legal action is necessary.

Consider Therapy

If your feelings after the flash mob event are overwhelming and interfering with your daily life, consider seeking professional help. A therapist or counselor can provide you with coping strategies and support to help you manage your emotions.

Conclusion

Coping with the aftermath of a flash mob event can be challenging, but with the right support and strategies, you can begin to heal and move forward. It's essential to recognize the impact of the event on your mental and emotional well-being, seek support, take care of yourself physically and mentally, understand your rights, document the event, and consider therapy if necessary. Remember that healing takes time, but with patience and self-care, you can recover from this traumatic experience.

CONCLUSION

In this book, we have explored the various risks and hazards associated with unpredictable events such as riots, protests, looting, and flash mobs. We have also discussed strategies for preparing for and staying safe during these events, as well as coping with their aftermath. While it is impossible to predict and prevent all unpredictable events, taking proactive measures and being prepared can go a long way in minimizing risks and ensuring safety.

As we have seen, there are several common risks and hazards associated with unpredictable events. These include physical violence, property damage, theft, and injury. Understanding these risks and hazards is the first step in preparing for and staying safe during unpredictable events. By being aware of potential dangers, individuals can take proactive measures to avoid or minimize them.

Pre-planning is crucial when it comes to managing unpredictable events. This includes preparing an evacuation plan, identifying safe exit routes, and knowing emergency contact information. In Chapter 5, we discussed the importance of pre-planning for managing unpredictable events. By having a plan in place, individuals can act quickly and confidently in emergency situations.

In Chapter 6, we discussed the importance of having emergency contact information readily available. This includes having contact information for emergency services, family members, and friends. In the event of an emergency, quick access to this information can be lifesaving. We also discussed the importance of ensuring that this information is up to date and easily accessible.

Chapter 7 focused on preparing an evacuation plan. This includes identifying safe exit routes and knowing where to go in the event of an emergency. It is important to practice this plan regularly to ensure that it is effective and efficient. Having a well-planned evacuation route can save lives and prevent injuries during unpredictable events.

Chapter 8 provided tips for staying safe during unpredictable events. This includes staying informed about potential risks and hazards, avoiding confrontation with violent individuals, and seeking safety in a group or with law enforcement if possible. By following these tips, individuals can minimize risks and stay safe during unpredictable events.

Chapters 9 through 11 provided strategies for staying safe during specific unpredictable events. Chapter 9 discussed strategies for staying safe during riots and protests, including identifying safe exit routes, avoiding confrontation, and seeking safety in a group. Chapter 10 discussed tips for protecting oneself during a looting event, including securing property, staying aware of one's surroundings, and avoiding confrontation with looters.

Chapter 11 provided strategies for staying safe during flash mobs. This includes avoiding areas where flash mobs are likely to occur, staying aware of one's surroundings, and seeking safety in a group or with law enforcement if possible. By following these strategies, individuals can minimize risks and stay safe during flash mobs.

In the aftermath of unpredictable events, it is important to take steps to recover and cope with the aftermath. Chapters 13 through 16 discussed strategies for dealing with the aftermath of unpredictable events. Chapter 13 emphasized the importance of being prepared for the aftermath by having emergency supplies and resources readily available. This includes having first aid kits, food, water, and other essential items on hand.

Chapter 14 discussed strategies for dealing with the aftermath of riots and protests. This includes assessing property damage, reporting any crimes, and seeking counseling or support as needed. Chapter 15 focused on recovering after a looting event. This includes contacting insurance companies, assessing property damage, and taking steps to secure property in the future.

Chapter 16 provided strategies for coping with the aftermath of flash mobs. This includes seeking counseling or support as needed and taking steps to prevent future incidents. By following these strategies, individuals can recover and cope with the aftermath of unpredictable events.

In conclusion, staying safe during unpredictable events requires proactive measures and careful planning.

Stay calm and avoid provoking the crowd. Do not engage in any aggressive behavior or make any gestures that could be interpreted as confrontational.

Try to move away from the crowd as quickly and safely as possible. Look for any exits, side streets, or safe areas where you can wait until the situation calms down.

Stay aware of your surroundings at all times. Keep an eye out for any potential danger and be prepared to take evasive action if necessary.

If you cannot leave the area, find a safe place to take cover. Look for any barriers or objects that can provide protection, such as a building or a parked car.

Stay in touch with friends and family members. Let them know where you are and what is happening, so they can stay informed and assist you if needed.

Follow the instructions of law enforcement officers or other authorities on the scene. If they tell you to move or take shelter, do so immediately.

Do not share any personal information or engage in any conversations with strangers or members of the crowd. Keep your focus on staying safe and getting out of the area as quickly as possible.

If you are injured or require medical attention, seek help as soon as possible. Call emergency services or look for any medical personnel or first responders on the scene.

Avoid posting any photos or videos of the incident on social media. This could potentially escalate the situation and put yourself or others in danger.

Once you are safely away from the scene, take time to reflect on the experience and seek any necessary support or counseling to help you process any trauma or stress caused by the incident.

THANKS FOR READING

REMEMBER   AN OUNCE OF PREVENTION IS WORTH A POUND OF CURE